A Character Building Book™

Learning About Charity from the Life of
Princess Diana

Caroline M. Levchuck

The Rosen Publishing Group's
PowerKids Press™
New York

To Rosemarie . . . Ever a Lady, Always a Friend
Special thanks to Nancy Ellwood and Danielle Primiceri for allowing me to meddle.

For information about the Diana, Princess of Wales Memorial Fund, please contact:
The Diana, Princess of Wales Memorial Fund, Millbank Tower, 2nd Floor, London, SW1P 4QP, United Kingdom

Published in 1999 by The Rosen Publishing Group, Inc.
29 East 21st Street, New York, NY 10010

First Edition

Book Design: Erin McKenna

Photo Credits: p. 4 © Reuters/John Stillwell/Archive Photos; pp. 7, 8, 11, 19, 20 © Express Newspapers/ Archive Photos; p. 12 © Reuters/Dylan Martinez/Archive Photos; p. 15 © P. A. News Ltd./Archive Photos; p. 16 © Express Newspapers/Michael Dunlea/Archive Photos.

Levchuck, Caroline M.
    Learning about charity from the life of Princess Diana / by Caroline M. Levchuck.
        p.   cm. — (A character building book)
    Includes index.
    Summary: A simple biography of Diana, Princess of Wales, emphasizing her charitable work for such causes as sick children, people with AIDS, and the elimination of land mines.
    ISBN 0-8239-5344-0
    1. Diana, Princess of Wales, 1961–1997—Juvenile literature. 2. Princesses—Great Britain— Biography—Juvenile literature. 3. Charity—Juvenile literature. [1. Diana, Princess of Wales, 1961–1997. 2. Princesses. 3. Charity.] I. Title. II. Series.
DA591.A45D537 1998
361.7—dc21
                                      98-22111
                                      CIP
                                      AC

Manufactured in the United States of America

Contents

The People's Princess

Princess Diana was one of the most famous women of the 20th century. During her lifetime, people all over the world fell in love with the Princess of Wales. It's no secret why. Her **compassion** (kum-PA-shun) and her drive to help adults and children in need made people everywhere look up to her and want to be like her. A princess and a mother, she was best known for her sense of **charity** (CHA-rih-tee).

◄ *Princess Diana will always be known for her generosity, kindness, and beauty.*

Lady in Waiting

Diana, Princess of Wales, was born Lady Diana Frances Spencer on July 1, 1961, in England. Both her parents were connected to the **royal** (ROY-ul) family. She had two older sisters and a younger brother. When Diana finished school she passed up a carefree life of fun with her friends. Instead, she decided to work as a nanny for an American family. She also became a kindergarten teacher. This was one of the first ways in which Diana showed others how much she wanted to help children.

Diana always loved children and spent her life doing all she could to help them. ▶

A Princess

On February 24, 1981, it was announced that Charles, the Prince of Wales, and **heir** (AYR) to the throne of England, would marry Lady Diana. People all around the world liked this shy young woman right away. Charles and Diana were married on July 29, 1981. Over 1 billion people around the world watched the wedding on television. Over 600,000 people watched from the streets of London. People believed that Charles and Diana would be the future King and Queen of England.

◀ *Charles and Diana's wedding was like a fairy tale.*

A Royal Mother

Princess Diana and Prince Charles had two children. Prince William, or Wills, was born on June 21, 1982. Prince Henry, or Harry, was born on September 15, 1984. Even though she had only been part of the royal family for a few years, Princess Diana knew her sons would have different lives than other boys their age. So she often broke **tradition** (truh-DIH-shun) by bringing Wills and Harry with her when she traveled. Diana took them to fun places too, such as Walt Disney World and McDonald's.

Princess Diana took the princes to a special circus called the Cirque du Soleil. ▶

A New Life

Charles and Diana loved their sons very much, but they weren't very happy in their marriage. They **separated** (SEH-puh-ray-ted) in December 1992 and were **divorced** (dih-VORST) in August 1996. Diana was still treated as a member of the royal family. Even though she would never be Queen of England, Diana told people that she simply wanted to be "the queen of people's hearts." Diana became just that by giving her time and attention to **charities** (CHA-rih-teez) around the world.

◄ *Princess Diana seemed to know just how to touch a child to make him or her smile.*

A Voice for Many

Because people watched Princess Diana's every move and listened to every word she said, she knew that she could use her fame to help others. After her divorce, Princess Diana **auctioned** (AWK-shund) off 79 of her beautiful gowns. The money raised—over 3.25 million dollars—was given to charities. Princess Diana also continued to be the **patron** (PAY-trun) of six charities, including the Hospital for Sick Children, Great Ormond Street. Most of the charities Diana supported help homeless young people and sick children and adults.

Diana brought hope to sick children at Great Ormond Street by raising money and spreading cheer. ▶

Kid Stuff

From her days as a teacher to the love she showed her two sons, Princess Diana had always tried to help kids. She met with children suffering from painful diseases such as **leprosy** (LEH-pruh-see). She served food to hungry children in Africa. And whenever Princess Diana visited sick children, she was sure to hug them and talk with them. Diana hoped that a visit from a kind and caring princess could help heal a child's heart. People saw what Princess Diana was doing and gave money to help these kids.

◀ *Princess Diana had a special way of making young people feel at ease around her.*

Angel of Mercy

For over ten years Princess Diana shared her charity by working to help people suffering from AIDS. In fact, when little was known about AIDS and how people got it, many people were afraid of those who had AIDS. Princess Diana helped change the way people treated children and adults with AIDS. In 1987, she shook hands with a man who had AIDS without worrying about getting sick. And she didn't stop there. For years to come, Princess Diana warmly hugged and held hands with many people suffering from AIDS.

Princess Diana was often called the Angel of Mercy because of the many times she visited sick people in hospitals. ▶

The World Was Watching

In the year before her death, the Princess worked to end the making and use of **land mines** (LAND MYNZ). Land mines have killed or injured more than 1 million people since 1975. Many of these people were children. When a child in a poor village is hurt by a mine, there is little hope that he or she will be able to get the best medical care. Princess Diana visited the countries of Angola and Bosnia, where land mines are still buried in the ground. The Princess spoke out to the whole world against the use of land mines.

By traveling to countries with land mines,
◀ *Princess Diana helped raise money for*
Mine Awareness projects everywhere.

Queen of Hearts

Sadly, Diana died at the age of 36 in a car accident on August 31, 1997. After her sudden death, the Diana, Princess of Wales, Memorial Fund was started. The purpose of the fund is to remember the life of the Princess and to support the charities she worked to help. In the first few weeks following her death, the fund got **donations** (doh-NAY-shunz) of almost 16 million dollars. Although Princess Diana is gone, her **legacy** (LEH-guh-see) of charity lives on in the memories of her that we carry in our hearts.

Glossary

auction (AWK-shun) A public sale at which goods are sold to the person who pays the most.

charities (CHA-rih-teez) Organizations that give relief to the needy.

charity (CHA-rih-tee) Generosity to people in need.

compassion (kum-PA-shun) Kindness toward others.

divorce (dih-VORS) When a couple ends their marriage.

donation (doh-NAY-shun) A gift, usually of money.

heir (AYR) A person inheriting something.

land mine (LAND MYN) A bomb buried underground during a war to prevent people from crossing over certain areas of land.

legacy (LEH-guh-see) Something left behind by a person's actions.

leprosy (LEH-pruh-see) A disease of the skin that can cause nerve damage, paralysis, and deformity of the limbs.

patron (PAY-trun) A person who lends her name to a group or organization to show that she supports it.

royal (ROY-ul) Relating to a king, queen, or royal family.

separated (SEH-puh-ray-ted) When a couple lives apart from each other for a certain period of time.

tradition (truh-DIH-shun) Something that is passed down through a culture.

Index